The Llama

A Dillon Remarkable Animals Book

The lama

By Gail LaBonte

P DILLON PRESS, INC.
Minneapolis, Minnesota 55415

Acknowledgments

I owe many thanks to Andrea Rowland of Walnut Creek, California, for providing me with valuable information and the pleasure of meeting the llamas of Blackwood Farms. She read the first draft of the manuscript for accuracy and gave me helpful comments.

I am also grateful to Sue and Steve Rolfing of the International Llama Association for the information they gave me in numerous pamphlets and during telephone conversations.

The photographs are reproduced through the courtesy of Rod Allin/Tom Stack & Associates; D. Donne Bryant, Virginia Ferrero, and Suzanne L. Murphy/D. Donne Bryant Photography; Breck P. Kent; Gail LaBonte; Inge Martin; and Steve Rolfing/Great Northern Llama Company. Cover: Steve Rolfing/Great Northern Llama Company.

Library of Congress Cataloging-in-Publication Data

LaBonte, Gail.
The llama / by Gail LaBonte.
(A Dillon remarkable animals book)
Includes index.
Summary: Describes the physical characteristics, habits, and natural environment of the llama. Also includes information on its history and relationship to people.
ISBN 0-87518-393-X
1. Llamas—Juvenile literature. [1. Llamas.] I. Title. II. Series.
QL737.U54L32   1989
599.73′6—dc 19   88-16407
                                                              CIP
                                                              AC

Dillon Press, Inc., 242 Portland Avenue South
Minneapolis, Minnesota 55415

Printed in the United States of America
1 2 3 4 5 6 7 8 9 10 98 97 96 95 94 93 92 91 90 89

Contents

2838

Facts about the Llama

Scientific Name: *Llama glama*

Range: Native to high plateaus of the central Andes Mountains in South America; many are being raised in North America

Description:

Height—At shoulder, 40 to 45 inches (102 to 114 centimeters); at head, 5 to 6 feet (1.5 to 1.8 meters)

Weight—300 to 450 pounds (136 to 205 kilograms)

Physical Features—Long neck and ears; small head with large eyes and split upper lip; thick wool on body and neck; two-toed foot with soft foot pad; three-chamber stomach for storing food as cud

Color—White, brown, or black, with many shades and combinations of color

Distinctive Habits: Are social, herd animals and need the company of other llamas; have a gentle and curious nature; are intelligent and easily trained; make a variety of sounds including a soft hum and a shrill alarm call; when angry, may spit, usually at other llamas

Food: Bunch grasses and shrubs, alfalfa hay, and oats

Reproductive Cycle: Females have a single "cria" or baby llama about eleven and one-half months after mating. The baby llama weighs 18 to 35 pounds (8.2 to 16 kilograms). It is weaned from the mother's milk at about 5 months of age.

Life Span: About 20 years

Uses: Llamas have been used as pack animals for thousands of years in South America, and they are still used that way today in both North and South America. Their wool can be sheared or combed and used to make cloth, rope, or yarn for knitting. Llamas are easy to raise and make good pets.

Chapter 1

An Amazing Animal

On farms and ranches from New York to California and north into Canada and Alaska, a curious-looking animal grazes peacefully. As it feeds, it hums happily. Large eyes, long ears and neck, and thick wool make this animal easy to tell apart from horses and cows. It is easy to care for, and has a gentle nature, making it fun to raise. Its soft wool can be made into beautiful warm sweaters and blankets. Yet it is also a strong and tough animal that can carry heavy packs on rocky paths and steep slopes in the wilderness where horses cannot go. This amazing creature is the llama.

The llama (pronounced *LAH-mah* or *YAH-mah*) comes from South America where it was **domesticated***, or tamed for use by people, thousands of

*Words in **bold type** are explained in the glossary at the end of this book.

9

years ago. In North America, people are raising llamas in many of the United States and Canadian provinces. In fact, llamas have become so popular that there aren't enough for everyone who would like to have one. Someday there may even be as many llamas as there are horses.

Since they are between 5 and 6 feet (1.5 to 1.8 meters) tall at the top of their heads, llamas may look as big as horses. But they are really much smaller, about the size of a large deer. They weigh half as much as most horses, and at the shoulder are about the height of a five- or six-year-old child. Still, their long necks and woolly bodies make them look larger and heavier than they are.

Like horses, llamas come in many colors. They can be white, black, or many shades of brown and gray. Some llamas are one solid color. Others have a "paint" pattern, brown or black with patches of white. **Appaloosas** are white with small, scattered spots of black or brown. A **calico** llama has black, brown, orange, and white patches mixed together.

Because of its long, woolly neck, the llama appears larger than its real size.

The huge eyes and "banana ears" of this llama stand out in a close-up view.

The llama has huge eyes with long, thick eyelashes. Like a deer, its face is narrow, and its nose and lips are soft. The llama's long ears come in three shapes. "Banana ears" curve inward over the head. "Tipped ears," which fold over at the tips, may be caused by frostbite after birth during a cold winter. "Wooly ears" are covered with long fur.

The llama's legs seem especially long and skinny next to its woolly body. When llamas move, they bring both legs on the same side of the body forward together. This way of moving, called **pacing**, requires a good sense of balance. A llama's top pacing speed is about twenty miles (thirty-two kilometers) per hour.

Llamas move in other ways, too. When they are going up a steep hill, they may walk like a horse, moving opposite fore and hind limbs together. When they are feeling frisky, or when male llamas are trying to impress females, they may jump up into the air, stiff-legged like a deer.

People and llamas usually get along well together. When someone comes to see them on a farm or ranch, these curious animals come from all parts of the pasture to gather around the visitor. Llamas like to sniff anything new. They may even put their soft lips against the visitor's cheek or blow softly into his or her face. This is the llamas' way of saying "hello."

A llama and its human owner share a happy moment—face to face.

Llama Language

The llama has an interesting language. It communicates with its body as well as its voice. In fact, watching a llama's ears can help a person understand its language.

Ears up and forward show alertness and curiosity. Ears back, but not down, mean nothing

The position of this llama's ears—up and forward—show it is alert and curious.

interesting is happening. The llama is just relaxing. Sometimes a llama will hold its ears to the side like airplane wings when it is listening to something from behind. When a llama's ears are down and close to its neck, the llama is annoyed or frightened. If the llama lays its ears down and tilts its head up, pay attention. It is mad and may spit.

Llamas don't spit often, and usually only at other llamas in arguments about food. Mostly, they spit just what is in their mouths, such as saliva and grass. But if they are really mad, they will bring up some food from their stomach, or **cud**, and spit it. What a smelly mess that makes!

Like cows, llamas chew their cud. A cow's stomach has four parts, but the llama's stomach has just three. The food is partly digested in the first stomach, and then the cud is brought back up for the llama to chew again. Chewing it a second time helps the llama get all the **nutrients** possible from its food.

Llamas also use their necks to communicate. When they are young, they sometimes wrestle with their necks. A llama lays its neck over another llama's neck and tries to push it down into a kneeling position. Females stop neck wrestling after they are a year old, but males continue all their lives. In this way they show their standing among the males of the herd. If they are really fighting,

These Peruvian llamas are having a fight.

not just playing, they may also bite another llama's neck or legs.

Llamas that don't want to fight use a **submissive posture**. This is a way of saying to a bigger llama, "Okay, I know you're the boss." Often a young male llama does this in front of an adult male. The youngster bends its neck down so its head is at the level of its back. The llama's ears point in an airplane wing position, and its tail curls forward on its back.

Listening to Llamas

Llamas express themselves with a variety of sounds, too. One of the sounds they make is a soft hum like a cat's purr, but louder. Air passing in and out of the llama's long throat creates the humming. In South America, people call this sound "praying," and it usually means that the llama is content or happy. Llamas often "pray" when they are grazing.

If the hum starts low but rises in pitch to a

whine, it means the llama is curious or alarmed about something. Llamas make this sound when they meet strange llamas or other animals such as elk or deer. If the hum is low and angry-sounding, it may be a threat, and spitting may follow. A series of short, high bleats that sound like a toy horn on a bike mean the llama is upset. Mothers and babies may make these sounds when they are first separated from each other.

When llamas are really frightened, they make a high-pitched sound like a donkey braying. Andy Tillman, a llama expert, describes it as a *nyerk* sound repeated over and over.

Male llamas may snort like a horse when they see a new llama or a female. The snort is probably a challenge, and females may answer the snort with a soft clicking sound. Their cheeks blow in and out as if they are blowing bubbles. When a male is put in a pasture with a female, it may make a noise that sounds like an *orgle*. Tillman describes this sound as an outboard motor boat going at slow speed.

Getting to know llamas and their language is fun. Most people who watch, listen, and spend time with these remarkable creatures say they are very special animals. Though llamas first arrived in North America only a century ago, they are not exactly newcomers to the continent. In the distant past, the llama's wild ancestors lived in the area many North Americans now call home.

A mother and baby llama make sounds to communicate with each other.

Chapter 2

At Home in the Mountains

Llamas have a long and interesting history. They are members of the camel family, the **camelids**. When people think of camels, they usually think of the Sahara Desert in North Africa. And yet, camels first lived in North America.

Many millions of years ago, the first camels, which were small animals, roamed the North American plains. During the ice ages, some camels **migrated** across the Bering Strait from Alaska to Siberia in Asia. Over time, these camels changed in many ways. They **evolved** into the large, two-humped Bactrian camel of Asia and the one-humped Arabian camel of North Africa. Other camels migrated south across Central America to South America. These were the ancestors of the llama.

A South American llama carries a load of straw.   23

Relatives of the Llama

The South American branch of the camel family has four kinds, or **species**, of animals. Two species, the **vicuña** and the **guanaco**, are wild animals. The llama and the **alpaca** were tamed for people's use. Today, there are no wild llamas or alpacas.

The four South American camelids live in the Andes, a mountain range that runs the length of South America near the west coat. Their **habitat** is the high plains, or **altiplano**, in Peru, Bolivia, Chile, and Argentina. Even though the altiplano lies near the equator, it does not have a hot climate. At 12,000 to 14,000 feet (3,657 to 4,267 meters), the weather remains cool or cold throughout the year. Plants do not grow well, and the region is almost treeless. The llama and its relatives feed on bunch grasses and other small plants.

"Truck of the Andes"

Scientists are not certain when the llama was first domesticated. They think it was between 4,000

A herd of llamas feeds on the altiplano, the plains of the Andes Mountains.

and 6,000 years ago. Since then the llama has provided many important items for the people of the Andes. The llama, along with the guinea pig, supplied most of their meat. They used its hide for shelter, shoes, sandals, and bags. They made candles from the llama's fat, rope and clothing from its wool, and tools from its bones. Its droppings, small

Llamas in a small caravan carry loads past an ancient Inca fort.

pellets like deer droppings, were burned for fuel.

Of all the needs the llama filled, carrying goods was the most important. Until the Spanish came, the people of the Andes did not use any wheels. The llama was and still is the "truck of the Andes," carrying goods back and forth between the high-lands and the lowlands.

From 1200 to 1532 A.D., the Incas created a powerful and wealthy empire and ruled the central Andes. During this time, llamas carried trading goods and military supplies over an advanced system of roads and bridges. Hundreds of llamas made up a single trade caravan. Thousands of llamas were used to haul ore from silver and gold mines. In fact, llamas were so important to the Incas that most of these animals belonged to the government.

Llamas still provided meat during the time of the Incas. Called **charqui**, the meat was cut into strips and dried. The word *jerky*, used to describe a kind of dried meat, comes from charqui.

Llamas were also important in Inca ceremonies. A white llama dressed in gold earrings, a red shirt, and a red seashell necklace walked before the ruler whenever he traveled. Some llamas were killed as a sacrifice to the Inca gods. When the people needed help with crops, they sacrificed black llamas. White llamas were offered to the sun god,

brown llamas to the god of creation, and spotted ones to the god of thunder. Even today, people of the Andes decorate llamas and march them around their fields to bring a healthy crop.

Llamas played an innocent part in the end of the Inca empire. When Atahualpa, the last Inca ruler, was captured by the Spaniards, he offered to fill his prison cell with gold in exchange for his life. Hundreds of llamas carried the gold from all parts of the empire. The Spaniards accepted the gold, but did not keep their promise to free Atahualpa. They kept him prisoner and later killed him.

Llamas have been important to the people of South America for many centuries. Yet the first of these remarkable animals did not arrive in North America until about one hundred years ago.

Roland Lindemann and William Randolph Hearst brought the first llamas to North America in the late 1800s. Most of these llamas were exhibited in zoos and animal parks. In the 1930s, no more llamas were allowed into the United States

A llama balances on a steep, rocky slope leading up to Machu Picchu, the site of an ancient Inca city.

because government officials feared they might bring foot-and-mouth disease into this country. This dangerous disease spreads easily among cows, horses, sheep, and many other animals.

Today, there are 12,000 to 15,000 llamas in the United States and Canada. Most are descendants of the animals Lindemann and Hearst brought to North America. Only a small number of llamas are displayed in zoos and animal parks. Almost all are pets and companions and pack and show animals for the people who raise them all over the continent.

Today, the people of the high plains of the Andes still depend on the llama to carry loads over the steep mountain trails.

In Montana's scenic Flathead Valley, a dog rests by a baby llama in front of the adult llamas of the herd.

Chapter 3

Living with Llamas

In North America, many owners consider llamas easier to raise than cattle, horses, pigs, or sheep. Their needs for food, shelter, and care are simple. Beyond these physical needs, llamas also need companionship.

Since llamas are social, herd animals, they like to live with others of their kind. A llama by itself is usually unhappy. People who raise llamas often sell them only in pairs, so they will have a companion. If an owner has just one llama, a sheep or a gentle dog should keep it company.

Food and Water

Llamas do not eat much. A full-grown llama needs only 6 to 12 pounds (2.7 to 5.4 kilograms) of hay each day. One acre (.4 hectares) of good pasture land is enough to feed four adult llamas.

Llamas are both **grazers** and **browsers**. As grazers, they eat grass and weeds that grow close to the ground, and as browsers, they eat the leaves from shrubs and bushes. Llamas have no front teeth on their upper jaw. Instead, they have a hard, bony gum. They use their front lower teeth and their flexible upper lip to grasp plants and break them off.

In South America, llamas eat many different kinds of plants in order to get enough to eat. In North America, though, llamas eat so much food that they sometimes become too fat. Alfalfa hay and oats are much richer than the llamas' native food. Eating too much of these foods can cause a weight problem that may be dangerous to the animals' health. Along with good pasture land and a controlled amount of alfalfa and oats, llamas need vitamin and mineral **supplements** to stay healthy.

Although they are relatives of the camel and

Llamas feed in a pasture in Ecuador, South America.

do not need much water, llamas cannot go for long periods without it. They need fresh, clean water available whenever they want to drink.

Shelter

A three-sided shed with a roof is enough to protect llamas from the rain and wind. Their thick wool keeps them warm through the worst kinds of weather. Since too much heat can be hard on them, they need shade trees or other cool places to escape from the hot sun. During very hot weather, they enjoy cooling off under sprinklers or in rubber wading pools.

Since llamas are not fence jumpers, a four-foot (1.2-meter) fence is enough to keep them in. Many owners, though, put up a higher fence to keep other animals, especially dogs, out. Llamas don't lean against fences and knock them down the way horses do. That means a fence for llamas does not have to be as strong as a fence for a horse pasture.

Along with a fence, owners often build a **catch**

A fenced-in pasture in Montana's Flathead Valley.

pen, a place to catch their animals. In this area, often a fenced-in corner of the pasture, llamas can be trained, examined, and observed at close range. Some owners place a movable fence on one side of the animal's shed and use it for a catch pen.

Llamas are neat animals that drop their pellets in communal **dung** piles. There are usually four or five piles scattered about in a field. When a llama smells llama droppings, it adds its droppings to the pile. It's important to keep the llamas' shelter free of droppings, so they don't start a dung pile in it.

Having Babies

At two years old, female llamas are mature enough to become mothers. After mating with a male llama, eleven and a half months pass before the baby is born. Llamas have only one baby at a time. Usually, it is born in daylight. In the cold Andes, being born during the warmer daytime hours gives the newborn llama a better chance to survive. In South America, people call the baby llama a **cria**, and many North Americans use this word, too.

Since the mother delivers her baby standing up, the cria's first experience in this world is a drop on the hard ground. Fortunately, it arrives feet first. Within fifteen minutes, the baby sits upright. Within thirty minutes, it stands up and enjoys its first meal of mother's milk.

A baby llama in the Peruvian Andes.

While its mother grazes, a baby llama enjoys its own meal of mother's milk.

Llama mothers and babies are best left to themselves to get to know one another. If crias are bottle-fed and handled too much, they may be difficult to train as adults. At five or six months of age, when a baby llama no longer needs its mother's milk, it is called a **weanling**. This is a good time to begin some training.

Training

Llamas are much calmer and easier to work with than horses or mules, and can be trained in a short time. Since llamas are naturally curious, just walking into the pasture may bring a weanling to the trainer. If the trainer walks into the catch pen, the llama may follow. After giving it a bucket with some alfalfa or oats, the trainer sits quietly. Stroking the animal's neck and face helps the llama become used to a human touch.

Now the llama is ready for a **halter**. This device has two straps that go around the nose and head of the llama, and a place to attach a lead rope. First, the trainer sets the halter near the weanling's food, so that the straps become a familiar sight. When the llama is ready, the trainer traps it in a corner, and slips the halter over its head.

After the weanling is comfortable wearing the halter, a lead rope can be attached. The first time the trainer tries to lead the llama, it will either buck, run, or lie down. If it bucks or runs, the trainer runs ahead, showing the animal that a person should be in front. If it kneels down, another person stands beside it, clapping loudly while the trainer says "up" and tugs on the lead rope. When the llama is ready to follow, the trainer leads it around obstacles such as trees or rocks.

At this point the weanling is too small for pack training, but old enough for people to begin handling its feet. Since the llama's feet are quite sensitive to touch, it will not like having them handled at first.

The foot of a llama has two toes with nails that never stop growing. In the Andes, the nails are likely to be worn down by walking on hard, rocky ground. On the soft pastures of North America, though, the nails can grow too long and cause problems. If this happens, they need to be clipped.

Because the llama may kick when its legs are first touched, the trainer sometimes starts by running a broom handle up and down the legs. Then the trainer gently picks up each front leg and han-

42   The foot of a llama has two toes with nails that never stop growing.

dles the animal's feet. Since the llama is more likely to kick when its hind legs are handled, a soft rope with a loop may be used to lift each hind leg the first few times. It is easier to start handling the llama's feet when it is young than when it is fully grown.

Llamas are not ready to carry packs until they are nearly two years old. Only male llamas are trained to carry packs, because females at this age are usually pregnant or nursing babies.

The pack bags used in South America, called **costals**, are large flat sacks woven from llama wool. Once they are filled, they are laid across the llama's back with equal weight on each side. Then they are tied on with a **soga**, a rope made of llama wool. North Americans also use the traditional costals or more modern packs made of nylon with side pockets. The pockets make it easy to get things out without unloading the llama.

Young llamas start with light packs. When they are fully grown, at about four years old, they can carry 55 to 65 pounds (25 to 30 kilograms) for 9 to 12 miles (15 to 20 kilometers).

Pack training a llama does not take long—even an adult llama can join a pack trip after only a week's training. After the llama has been haltered and tied to a fence, the trainer places a saddle pad or empty costal on its back. Later, the trainer gradually adds weight to the pack. The weight must be equal on both sides of the animal, and the pack must never be too heavy. Soon the llama is ready for a pack trip.

Chapter 4

For Fun and Profit

Llamas make wonderful companions on long hikes into the wilderness. Carrying burdens was what llamas were bred to do thousands of years ago. Some South Americans call llamas "speechless brothers" because they carry the burdens of their human companions without complaining.

Besides being easy to train, llamas have many advantages over horses and mules. In wilderness areas, llamas don't do much damage to trails or plants. They weigh much less than horses, and the bottom of their foot is a soft pad like the palm of a person's hand. Horses, which have hard hoofs and heavy bodies, churn trails into deep dust.

Llamas are sure-footed animals. Their two-toed feet walk easily over rocky paths and slippery

High in the Montana mountains, people and llamas follow a wilderness trail along the Swan Divide.   47

A backpacker and llamas in a mountain meadow near Glacier National Park.

slopes. In fact, they have carried equipment for forest crews where horses could not go.

Transporting llamas to the wilderness is not difficult, either. Because of their size and weight, they fit in small trailers. They can also ride in the back of a covered pickup truck or a van. One llama even joined children on a school bus ride.

On a trail, llamas are curious about new animals. Their curiosity and keen eyesight allow their human companions to observe more wildlife. When a llama spots a deer, elk, or any other animal, it will stop and stare in that direction. People who follow the llama's gaze may see an animal they otherwise would have missed.

Llamas on their first pack trip are like children on their first long hike. They get tired and sore and lie down on the trail. But after they have hiked a few times in new areas, they are eager to go.

Making Money

On North American farms and ranches, llama owners make money by raising the animals and selling them. Since there are not enough llamas for all the people who want them, llamas may sell for as much as $15,000 each—the price of a prized Arabian horse!

Llamas also produce wool. Llama owners can clip the wool every two years before the llama

sheds, or they can comb the loose wool from the llama's coat at any time. Though llama wool has many uses in South America, most owners in North America collect the wool only for their own use. They spin it into yarn for knitting or weaving.

People Pleasers

Whether they are raising llamas to sell or to use on pack trips, most owners have fun with these animals. Llamas make great pets. They don't bark, destroy property, or leave messes in the neighbor's yard. Llamas have pulled carts of carolers at Christmastime, trick-or-treated at Halloween, carried gifts to birthday parties, and even helped a state senator campaign for office.

Throughout the United States and Canada, more and more llama shows are being held. At these shows, llamas are judged for their beauty as well as their performance. One of the most popular events is the obstacle course. In this contest, owners lead their llamas through gates and tun-

On a mountain trail, llamas often spot wild animals before their human companions see them.

nels, and across bridges and jumps. The llamas show their intelligence and training. There are also llama races in which owners jog alongside their animals. Children as well as adults participate with the llamas in these shows.

Being around llamas usually makes people feel happy and relaxed. The llamas' gentle behavior, soft fur, and contented hum are soothing. Many children have enjoyed visits to llama farms, and llamas have even visited people in nursing homes.

On farms and ranches, on wilderness trails and the high plains of the Andes, people and llamas have a very special relationship. In North America, as well as in their native land, llamas have become "speechless brothers" for their human companions. On both continents, these remarkable animals are now truly at home.

On Blackwood Farms in Walnut Creek, California, Christopher Rowland kneels alongside a llama in holiday dress.

Sources of Information about Llamas

Learning about llamas is fun, but meeting them is even better. To find out if there are llamas you can visit near your home, write to the International Llama Association or the other groups listed below. They can tell you about llama shows in your area and about people who lead llamas on pack trips into the wilderness. They may also have information about llama farms and ranches in your state.

International Llama Association
P.O. Box 37505
Denver, CO 80237

Llama Association of North America
P.O. Box 1174
Sacramento, CA 95806

Llamas Magazine
P.O. Box 100
Herald, CA 95638

Glossary

alpaca (al-PAK-uh)—a member of the camel family native to South America; domesticated to make use of its long, soft wool

altiplano (al-tih-PLAH-noh)—means "high plain" in Spanish; the plateau regions at elevations of 12,000 feet (3,657 meters) and higher in the central Andes Mountains

appaloosa (ap-uh-LOO-suh)—a pattern of coloring on horses and other animals in which small spots of brown or black are scattered across a white background

browsers (BROWZ-urz)—animals that feed on the leaves and twigs of bushes and trees

calico (KAL-uh-coh)—a mixture of black, reddish-brown, and white fur

camelids (KAM-uh-lihds)—animals that belong to the camel family

catch pen—a small, fenced-in area for catching llamas and livestock such as cows or horses

charqui (CHAHR-kee)—a word from the Quechua language used to mean strips of dried meat

costals (CAHST-uhlz)—large, flat sacks woven from llama wool, which are filled with goods and carried on a llama's back

cria (KREE-uh)—a Spanish word for a baby animal

cud—food that has been swallowed and partly digested and then brought back to the mouth for more chewing

domesticated (doh-MEHS-tuh-kay-tuhd)—used here to describe animals that have been tamed for use by humans

dung—waste matter from an animal's bowels; droppings

evolved (ee-VAHLVD)—changed gradually over long periods of time

grazers (GRAYZ-urz)—animals that feed on grass and other plants growing close to the ground

guanaco (gwuh-NAHK-oh)—a member of the camel family native to South America, especially Argentina; hunted for its meat, this wild animal is threatened with extinction (the death of all members of a species)

habitat—the place or area where a plant or animal lives naturally

halter—headgear used for controlling or leading an animal; it consists of a strap around the nose and a strap around the back of the animal's head

migrated—used here to refer to animals that moved from one region to another in search of food or a new homeland

nutrients (NOO-tree-ehnts)—the vitamins, minerals, proteins, and other substances in food that help support a living animal or plant

pacing—a way of moving in which an animal brings both legs on the same side forward together

soga (SOH-gah)—a rope made of llama wool that is used to tie a costal, or pack bag, on a llama

species (SPEE-sheez)—distinct kinds of individual plants or animals that have common characteristics and share the same scientific name

submissive (suhb-MIHS-ihv) posture—a body position an animal may use in front of a more powerful animal to show its place in the social order

supplements (SUHP-luh-mehnts)—a substance added to make up for what is missing; for instance, vitamin and mineral supplements are sometimes added to food

vicuña (vih-KOON-yuh or vy-KOON-yuh)—an untamed member of the camel family, native to the high elevations in the Andes Mountains of South America

weanling (WEEN-ling)—a young llama that no longer needs its mother's milk

Index